FIVE MEN UNDER ONE UMBRELLA

Joseph Low

5 MEN UNDER 1 UMBRELLA

& Other Ready-to-Read Riddles

MACMILLAN PUBLISHING CO., INC.
New York
COLLIER MACMILLAN PUBLISHERS
London

3   4   5   6   7   8   9   10

Library of Congress Cataloging in Publication Data
Low, Joseph, date   Five men under one umbrella.
(A Ready-to-read book)
1. Riddles.   [1. Riddles]   I. Title.
PZ8.7.L6Fi   398.8   74-20615   ISBN 0-02-761460-3

For 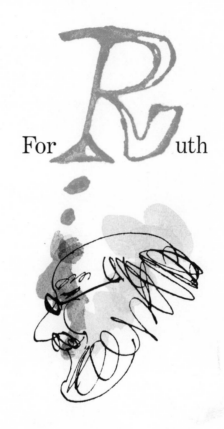uth

Five men

under one umbrella.

Why did none get wet?

It wasn't raining.

A goat, a boat,

a funny nose.

How can you spell them

without any o's?

them

How long should a man's legs be?

Long enough
to reach
the ground.

How can you spell candy
with only two letters?

C and Y

How would you like
to raise some strawberries?

With a spoon.

When is a girl
like a small bucket?

When she's a little pale.

What has ten legs

and catches flies?

A family of five swallows.

When is a boy like a pony?

When he's a little hoarse.

Who was the straightest man
in Old England?

The king—because he was a ruler.

Would you rather a lion

killed you or a tiger?

I'd rather he killed the tiger.

What is it

you can't name

without breaking it?

Silence.

What is it that is put on the table,
is usually cut, but is never eaten?

A pack of cards.

How many balls of string
would it take
to reach the moon?

Only one, if it were long enough.

What question can never
be answered by "Yes"?

Are

you

asleep?

What room has no walls,

no floor, no window, no door?

A mushroom.

How many raisin bran muffins
can the hairy monster eat
on an empty stomach?

Only one—
after that
his stomach
isn't empty.

The more you take away,

the larger it grows.

What is it?

A hole in the ground.

What coat has no sleeves,
no buttons, no front,
no back, and fits best
when put on wet?

A coat of paint.

If a man crossing a stream
on a log should fall,
what would he fall against?

Against his will.

On which side of the house
should you plant a rose bush?

The outside.

How is a mule different
from a postage stamp?

One you lick with a stick,

     the other you stick with a lick.

	DEC.	1	2	3	4
5	6	7	8	9	10	11
12	13	14	15	16	17	18
19	20	21	22	23	24	25
26	27	28	29	30	31	

Why is a calendar
like a Christmas pudding?

It has so many dates in it.

Why is an empty purse
always the same?

There is
never
any change
in it.

What state is round

on the ends

and high in the middle?

Why does a cook
never eat his apron?

Because it goes

against his stomach.

How did Jonah feel when
the whale swallowed him?

Rather down in the mouth.

What kind of driver
never gets arrested?

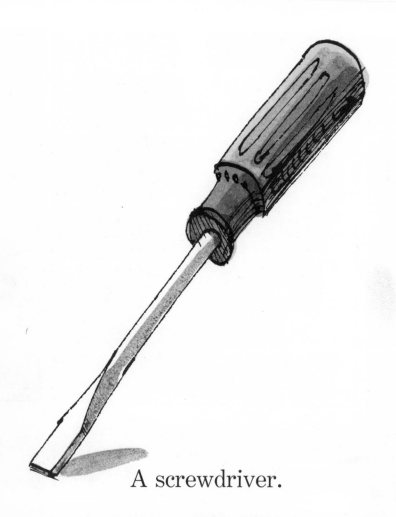

A screwdriver.

Which flowers should be
kept in the zoo?

The dandelion

and the tiger lily.

What is stranger than
a dog who can count?

A spelling bee.